Fighting Depression

How to Fight Depression and Be Happy Again

by Casey Belanger

Table of Contents

Introduction

Everyone has felt sad or blue at one point or another in their life. It is normal to have feelings like these, if they do not last long and pass within a few hours or days. While people might confuse these feelings with depression, it is important to recognize that depression is worse. Depression is actually a lasting disorder. It interferes with your day to day life, causing unbearable pain not only to you but also to those around you. Yet, despite this, a large percentage of people suffering from depression don't seek treatment, even though they could potentially be helped. Depression is ultimately treatable, so if you exhibit signs or symptoms of depression do not ignore the problem, hoping it will fade away.

There are several different forms of depression, including persistent depressive disorder and major depression. The former involves a depressed mood which would typically last for around two years. The latter is more severe, and very dangerous if not treated. People with persistent depressive disorder typically experience periods of less-severe symptoms at times which can degenerate into major depression along the way. The symptoms of persistent depressive disorder normally only last for two years or so, however major depressive disorder can bring your life to a halt. It can affect your ability to do anything constructive including eating, sleeping, working, or enjoying the different aspects of daily life.

If you are experiencing symptoms of depression, or know someone close to you who is, then this book will prove helpful in guiding you toward different treatments. Remember, depression is a deep-rooted disorder and therefore cannot be treated as quickly as drinking some Pepto Bismol to cure an upset stomach. Even still, it's important to approach this problem with a determined attitude – no matter how long it takes to get well, you should proceed forward with treatment until you feel normal again.

Let's get started!

Chapter 1: Causes of Depression

Finding the cause of depression can be difficult as there is often no specific cause. It can be hard to pinpoint any single reason for feeling so low; and therefore, it may be puzzling, trying to determine exactly what you should do to make things better for yourself. That's ok. The factors contributing to the development of this disorder vary from individual to individual, and therefore the best treatment approach may vary as well. The key is figuring out what solution works best for you, even if you can't understand what the cause may be.

Additionally, there are people who are simply more prone to depression than others. Depression can take a long time to develop in some cases. It could develop as a result of serious and unpleasant situations or events in a person's life or in other cases it might be hard even to trace the trigger. It is however important to know some of the risk factors. This makes treating the problem, and thus coming out of the dungeon of depression, potentially quicker than if you have no clue as to what could be causing you trouble. Below are some factors that are known to cause depression:

Events in your life: - According to researchers, it is possible for you to suffer depression if you are exposed to difficult situations continuously. Some of these events include cases of relationship abuse, long periods of unemployment, extended durations of stress exposure in business or the work-place, and long-term loneliness or isolation. These are more likely to trigger depression than recent and isolated stressful events. However, for people who are already at risk of being depressed – owing to personal factors or bad experiences in the past – recent cases of stress, including marital break-ups or losing a job, can trigger depression.

Personality: - People with certain personalities are simply more at risk of depression than others. This is especially so for those who are prone to low self-esteem, pessimism or negativity, those inclined to worry too much or to be overly-anxious, very thin-skinned people and those who are vulnerable to criticism, and perfectionists.

Family history: - Some people have an increased genetic risk, especially those for whom depression runs in the family. But this does not mean that you will get depressed simply because your family has a history. Even for people with increased genetic risks, a combination of other personal factors and life events will be needed to play a role in influencing the development of depression.

Brain chemicals: - Although it is not yet very clear how this happens, research has established that changes in chemicals in the brain could be the cause of depression. Studies have shown that changes in the activities and levels of certain chemicals such as dopamine, norepinephrine and serotonin can influence the development of this problem. Normally, these 3 chemicals are responsible for mood and motivation, and they help carry messages in the brain. If there are changes in stress hormone levels, the likelihood of getting depression is higher, especially if the changes are prolonged and untreated. Severe depression has commonly been associated with changes in brain chemistry, as opposed to moderate or mild depression, which will typically be based on things that have happened in a person's life.

Severe medical illnesses: - Chronic illnesses and/or pain have been associated with depression, especially when their treatment is long-term or ongoing. These can trigger depression directly or indirectly, especially when you are prone to anxiety, stress, and worry. Under this category, it's important to note that there are also cases of post-natal depression which, if not properly handled, can develop into more severe depression in women.

Drug abuse and alcoholism: - People who use drugs and alcohol are at much greater risk of getting depressed than those who do not. This is especially true if alcohol and drugs become a problem, as opposed to a one-time experience. If you have a substance use or abuse problem, it's important to deal with it head-on, even as you deal with the problem of depression, because the two go hand in hand.

As aforementioned, depression is normally triggered by a combination of different factors and therefore we cannot pinpoint a single factor as the sole cause of the problem. However, the good news is that there ARE SOLUTIONS for depression, typically in the form of therapy and medical treatment. Understanding the possible triggers for your depression is just the starting point.

Chapter 2: Signs and Symptoms of Depression

Symptoms of depression vary from one individual to another, and sometimes vary too with different cultures and genders. An aged person is likely to show different signs to those manifested by a teenager and this makes all the difference when it comes to diagnosing the problem. It should however be noted that some symptoms are shared commonly among all depressed people, since the problem is more emotional than physical. On top of this, it is worth noting that although the problem is emotional, most symptoms will manifest themselves physically, and that is something you should look out for.

One thing that is common among people suffering from depression is that they will find some of the easiest tasks, for example eating, showering, getting dressed, or even waking up tremendously difficult and taxing. So, don't be surprised if you find yourself unwilling to take a shower or have breakfast, as this is a common feeling in almost all cases of depression.

People who suffer from depression are always at risk of experiencing mood decline, which eventually results in a negative preconceived notion that informs all their experiences. Depression is normally associated with negative emotions such as fear, shame, anger, and worthlessness. These can be noticeable in the body through physical symptoms such as nausea, pains, aches, and other unpleasant feelings. It is also common for people with depression to feel weak, tense, or irritable, not to mention that they can also experience feelings of unexplained fatigue without relief. As the problem advances and develops, one can even begin to show no emotional expression whatsoever, or even eventually to begin to experience suicidal thoughts and behaviors. It is critical to take action immediately, as soon as you start to notice any symptom at all, so as not to let it get to a worse point.

Other signs and symptoms to look out for include:

Behavioral tendencies such as a lack of concentration, withdrawal from family and friends, disinterest in previously enjoyable activities and dependence on drugs and sedatives.

Physical problems such as feeling sickly and run-down, a churning stomach, muscle pains, headaches, insomnia, change or loss of appetite, and unexplained weight loss or gain.

Someone suffering from depression is also likely to experience unpleasant thoughts and feelings, which could include a sense of worthlessness, no desire to live, low self confidence, and even feeling as if they are a bother, and therefore others are better off without them.

However, the different signs and symptoms highlighted above could also be attributed to other disorders, and therefore it is important not to jump to conclusions too quickly. Whatever the case, it's best to consult with your doctor – and your therapist if you have one – at the earliest possible point to avoid worsening of the problem, and instead to have it resolved and remedied as soon as possible.

Chapter 3: Natural Remedies for Depression

Depression is therefore caused by a variety of different factors, sometimes in combination. In the same way, the treatment methods are varied and can be used together for management of depression. There is no single proven treatment that can be endorsed as a conclusive cure-all to depression, and in many cases your doctor will use different therapies and treatments in a complementary way to deal with the problem. A holistic approach is always most effective when dealing with depression.

Here are some Natural Treatment and Management Strategies:

Diet: - Although no single diet can help to treat depression outright, the food you eat can certainly help to stimulate your brain to produce hormones. These can help you feel good, boost your concentration, regulate your moods, improve sleep, and reduce anxiety. For example, cashews have been proven to increase happiness and decrease depression – similar to the antidepressant Prozac – simply due to its amino acid, known as "L-tryptophan", which is made into the neurotransmitter serotonin – making you feel mellow and at ease. Also try to consume plenty of antioxidants, to protect your body from destructive free radicals, including foods with Vitamin C (lemons, oranges, blueberries, kiwi, peppers, strawberries, etc.), Vitamin E (seeds and nuts, wheat germ, etc.), and beta-carotene (carrots, pumpkin, spinach, broccoli, cantaloupe, peaches).

Your diet should not only include the foods that are good for you, but should also restrict or reduce certain foods that are bad for you from your daily consumption. For example, studies have shown that foods with too much sugar can worsen your mood, making it important to reduce the amount of sugar you take in. Additionally, you should avoid or reduce the intake of alcohol and products containing caffeine, which can worsen depression symptoms such as insomnia, anxiety, and mood swings.

Instead, you should consider taking products or foods that contain vitamin B6, which helps in the production of the mood-enhancing neurotransmitters dopamine and serotonin. Also consider eating foods that are a good source of magnesium, including whole grains, fruits, green vegetables, nuts, and legumes. Magnesium is important since it helps in the production of serotonin. The body system is depleted of magnesium during times of stress and depression, meaning you should aim to replenish it.

Exercise: - Exercise can help to greatly improve your mood. For many years, physical exercise has been considered one of the best ways to manage depression. Exercising regularly helps the brain to produce and release chemicals responsible for mood elevation, while reducing stress hormones. The best thing with exercise is that you have a wide variety of activities to choose from, and therefore you can select a few to engage in on regular basis. For example, you can choose to visit a gym for 3 or 4 days a week, or opt for a brisk walk every morning for at least thirty minutes, five days each week. Additionally, you can jog, cycle, dance, or play tennis with friends. Exercising will not only help to improve your mood, but also keep you physically fit.

Take omega-3s: - Omega 3 fatty acids are essential in treating depression. They can be obtained from fish oils, or by consuming fish as part of your daily diet, or at least several times a week. Avocados also contain Omega 3. Additionally, Omega 3 is available in the form of pill or liquid supplements which you can take on a daily basis.

Chapter 4: Alternative Treatments for Depression

In addition to the natural treatments in the previous chapter, there are other alternatives that will go a long way in reducing the effects of depression. These include the following:

Relationships: - Although people with depression may exhibit symptoms of loneliness and want to be left in isolation, relationships can play a very important role as part of your treatment. Family and friends can help a lot in boosting your recovery as they offer support, a listening ear, good company, and just being there for you. Remember that recovery is hard to achieve in isolation. People suffering from depression should participate in social activities with people who love and care about them; even though this is the last thing they feel like doing. Staying close to people you love can work as a shield against symptom intensification while increasing your levels of confidence and wellbeing.

Relaxation training: - This is commonly used to treat cases of anxiety. It is important to know that anxiety precedes depression in many cases and that you can therefore often reduce depression simply by using relaxation training. This training helps relax tense muscles, while at the same time reducing anxious thoughts and behaviors. Relaxation training comes in different forms, including progressive muscle relaxation – which trains people to tense and relax particular groups of muscles through voluntary relaxation.

Online forums and support groups: - As with many other disorders, people with depression can come together to help each other by sharing their experiences. These groups often also invite people who have recovered from depression to share their own success stories and connect with those still experiencing the condition. This helps to demonstrate that recovery is possible, and just around the corner. Online forums are also available although in-person support groups are known to be more effective.

Mindfulness meditation and sleep: - Although people with depression can appear docile at times, the truth of the matter is that there is a lot going on in their minds and nerves. Learning to relax and sleeping adequately can help greatly in calming the nerves and mind, and in that way in can reduce the effects of depression. It is well-known that people with depression can experience worsening conditions if they do not sleep properly. Sleeping in proper conditions with minimal or no distractions will help to improve your quality of sleep, helping you to relax.

Meditation also helps in quieting the mind and relieving depression.

Bright light therapy: - Bright light treatment has been found to help reduce the severity of symptoms associated with depression. According to meta-analysis of this treatment, its effects are similar to those of conventional antidepressants. This therapy can be used alongside other treatments for maximized results, especially when used to treat seasonal depression.

It is worth noting that these natural remedies and alternative treatments are highly effective if used together with other treatment methods, but that they cannot necessarily be trusted to be as effective on their own. People suffering from depression should talk to their doctors to come up with the right combination of treatments. This is normally determined by the severity of symptoms and signs, and the type of depression will also determine the treatment used.

Chapter 5: Other Treatments for Depression

Although depression is a serious mental condition, it is worth noting that there are effective treatment methods available which can help to manage the problem. Unfortunately, many people with depression, and sometimes also their relatives, make the mistake of feeling ashamed about the problem. They therefore do not seek help from professionals which could otherwise help to overcome the depression and prevent the situation from worsening. Research shows that millions of American women and men suffer from depression and its effects every year. It is therefore important to know all of the treatment options available.

When seeking depression treatment, it is always important to understand that no one treatment is suited to everyone needs. However, with proper treatment, anyone can experience a considerable reduction of the symptoms related to this disorder. It is important to use therapy techniques, natural remedies and other alternative treatments available for depression before resorting to antidepressant medications. Below are some of the well-known therapies that can prove helpful in the recovery process, while at the same time preventing depression reoccurrence.

Cognitive behavior therapy (CBT)

Cognitive behavior therapy is designed to help people suffering from depression to understand how their cognition or thinking, and behavior or actions, affect their feelings. This treatment is highly respected and has been used to help people of many different ages and walks of life. Basically, CBT involves working with a professional therapist to scrutinize a pattern of existing thoughts and behaviors which are responsible for the development of depression, for worsening the situation or for hindering recovery.

The emphasis of CBT is on changing the person's thoughts and behavioral patterns by introducing a new way of thinking about certain problems or situations in life. By doing this, a depressed person will be able to shift from their negative thought patterns and actions to a more positive and practical problem-solving approach. During CBT therapy sessions, a professional therapist takes the depressed person through the process of identifying his or her own negative thoughts. They should then be able to more clearly see their own pattern of thinking. Once these negative thoughts are identified, the next step is to help develop a mechanism of challenging them, by making it understood that these negative thoughts are not realistic. With this in place, the depressed person will be able to replace his or her negativity with more positive and helpful thoughts.

The process is made complete through the second part of therapy, known as behavior therapy, which trains the person to develop the necessary skills and techniques to change their behavior or reaction towards life and various situations. For example, your therapist can work with you to help improve your communication skills and by so doing, you will be more confident in your social life. This helps in the reduction of depression signs and symptoms.

Psychoanalysis therapy

Psychoanalysis is a talk therapy which is normally used to stir up or bring about a person's unconscious emotions as well as experiences. This is typically done with the assumption that the source of psychological problems in the depressed person could be in their unconscious mind. There is therefore a need to reach in and resolve those deep-seated issues. A therapist will help the person to recognize those repressed or hidden emotions and thoughts, as a way of resolving them openly and conclusively. By reaching into these emotions and thoughts and dealing with them, a depressed person can move past them and enjoy a life of freedom and reduced depression symptoms.

Psychodynamic therapy

Psychodynamic therapy is very similar to psychoanalysis therapy. It too is designed to help a person suffering from depression to appreciate how unconscious emotions and unresolved issues can affect his or her behavior and feelings. The only difference between psychoanalysis and psychodynamic therapies is that the psychoanalysis digs deeper into those issues.

Interpersonal therapy or IPT

Interpersonal therapy appreciates that depression as a problem can result from, or be made worse by, difficulties in our daily relationships. It is therefore structured to focus on relationship problems, with the objective of developing the necessary skills that will help to deal with these problems. Interpersonal therapy is considered essential in helping people with depression to recognize any relationship patterns that could be making them more exposed. Identifying these patterns makes it easier to work towards improvement in their relationships, managing issues of grief and establishing new ways to relate with others properly. A therapist will use this therapy if he or she considers that the problem comes from relationships and related issues. Interpersonal therapy is brief, but focused, and will help to improve communication skills and techniques which can be used to resolve any interpersonal conflicts.

Experimental therapy

Experimental therapy is in a way similar to cognitive behavioral therapy, in that it helps train people to distinguish between harmful or misguided emotional responses and those which are healthier. This therapy adopts a more empathetic, supportive, patient-therapist relationship, as opposed to the strictly neutral relationship that characterizes the other types of depression therapies. Experimental therapy encourages this kind of a relationship because people are much more likely to get well, and feel better with time, when they feel understood and well treated.

Other therapies include online therapy or counseling, which encourages the use of avenues such as Skype, instant messaging, or other real time means of communication. While this does not allow for a one-on-one interaction between the person and their therapist, it is still pursued as a suitable option for many people, especially in the modern-day world.

Having highlighted the different types of therapies used in treating depression, it is worth noting that no single therapy can claim to be a "one-size-fits-all" for every depression disorder patient. It is clear that no one kind of treatment can be expected to produce exactly the same kind of effects on any two individual people. Therapy for depression can be administered in different forms including groups, individuals and even in a family set up. However, the most important thing is to find the right therapist and to commit to the process, while cooperating with your therapist for the best results. Always remember that depression therapy is not a quick fix for the problem and will therefore take some sessions before the desired results are seen. Committing to the sessions is very important.

Pharmaceutical drugs for treating depression

In addition to therapies, the use of pharmaceutical medicines has for years been used to treat depression. These drugs should however be used as a last resort and under the careful supervision of a qualified and licensed medical practitioner. It is important to understand that antidepressants have side effects and should only be used based on the symptoms exhibited by the depressed person. Additionally, different medicines are used to treat different types of depressions and therefore one must be careful when deciding on their usage. It is also important to avoid overdependence on these drugs.

Antidepressant drugs must not be considered to be a panacea or 'happy pills.' They should only be used by prescription and, if properly used, these drugs can help reduce depression symptoms amazingly. Their use is determined by the history of the disorder, its severity, personal preferences and the person's age. In most cases, antidepressants are used in combination with depression therapies.

How antidepressants work

In most cases, antidepressants are used to influence the rate at which certain chemicals (commonly known as neurotransmitters) are removed or produced in the brain. These chemicals include norepinephrine and serotonin, and are essential for normal functionality of the brain. These endogenous chemicals are also associated with the control of moods and other functions including sleep, pain, eating and thinking. The prescription of antidepressants is intended to help increase the production of these natural chemicals, making them available to the brain.

Certain forms of depression, such as psychosis and bipolar disorder, require the use of medication to treat. A single drug or a combination of two or more might be used, depending on a number of factors. Below are some of the commonly used drugs for depression treatment.

Types of antidepressants

• SSRI antidepressants, or Selective Serotonin Reuptake Inhibitors, include drugs such as Prozac (Fluoxetine), Citalopram (Celaxa), Escitalopram (Lexapro), Sertraline (Zoloft) and Paroxetine (Paxil). Essentially, these antidepressants are designed only to act on the neurotransmitter serotonin.

• SNRI antidepressants, or serotonin norepinephrine reuptake inhibitors, are designed to modulate both the serotonin and norepinephrine neurotransmitters. Some of the drugs in this category include Duloxetine (Cymbalta), Desvenlafaxine (Pristiq), Venlafaxine (Effexor and Effexor XR) and Milnacipran (Savella). These dual-acting drugs offer some depression sufferers greater advantages when compared to the SSRI antidepressants. However, this does not make them suitable for all people suffering from depression.

• Tricyclic antidepressants (tricyclics) have been used to treat depression cases for many years. The medication modulates several neurotransmitters including serotonin and related brain chemicals. These drugs include Amoxapine (Asendin), Doxepin (Silenor), Amitriptyline (Elavil, Levate), Protriptyline (Vivactil) and Clomipramine (Anafranil), among others.

Other types of antidepressants available on the market include Bupropion (Welbutrin), Mirtazapine (Remeron), and Venlafaxine (Effextor), among others. These medications modulate different chemicals in the brain and work differently from SSRIs and tricyclics.

Note

This list should not be used as a substitute for or supplement to the skills, expertise and knowledge of a professional healthcare provider. As has been mentioned, different treatment approaches are used to deal with cases of depression based on a host of factors. It is therefore important to talk with your doctor before buying or using these medications at any given time.

Chapter 6: Common Depression Myths Demystified

There are many myths and misconceptions surrounding depression. In many cases, the word "depressed" is used to describe a person going through a tough day, or someone experiencing bouts of bad mood. It is important to realize that everyone has low moments from time to time; this does not necessarily make them depressed. It is possible to feel down and 'depressed', but these feelings will typically disappear within a short period of time. However, in other people, these moods will extend for long periods and become worse, thus becoming a serious disorder, a medical depression. The most unfortunate thing when it comes to depression is that myths (misinformation) can cause people to feel isolated, or experience increased stigma. Below are some of the most common myths about depression, demystified.

1. Depression is having a bad mood or feeling deeply sad

The truth: - Deep sadness and bad mood can be symptoms accompanying depression. However, when these feelings are associated with clinical depression, they are bound to last for a long time – this could be a matter of weeks, months or even years. Clinical depression can begin with these bad feelings, owing to cases of grief or disappointment, but will eventually lead to a serious illness that requires treatment.

2. Depression is associated with aging, women and the weak

The truth: - Depression does not in any way discriminate based on gender, age or personality. It is good to know that some people are more prone to this mental disorder than others, especially women. However, anyone can become depressed, including men, although it is true that they typically take longer to show symptoms and signs. Both the young and aged people can suffer from depression although changes surrounding aging can make someone more prone to depression. However, depression is not a package that comes with aging or weakness. Even the greatest people in society can develop depression.

3. Depression means you are becoming crazy

The truth: - This laughable myth has been propagated for many years, thus making depression a shameful disorder which many are never willing to expose or seek help for. However, being depressed does not mean you are a cabbage case or are becoming insane. Although depression is a mental disorder, it is not true that it is a case of madness, and therefore it should not be treated as such.

4. People with depression are dangerous and suicidal

The truth: - Although many people consider depressed people to be dangerous to be around, depression does not necessarily make someone dangerous and suicidal. Depression can be managed properly and people should not be isolated out of fear of the myth above. Depressed people are normal and only need help to overcome the problem.

5. Depression can only be treated medically

The truth: - Although antidepressants have been used as a part of depression treatment, they are not the only cure for the disorder. In fact, many people are treated without using depressants, but with a combination of other natural treatments and therapies. Medical treatments are only a small percentage of the potential therapies which can be used.

6. Depression is hereditary

The truth: - Although many people fear they will get depression simply because their grandparents or parents had the problem, this disorder is not hereditary. There is only a very slightly increased likelihood of becoming depressed for those whose relatives have suffered with depression. One however could "inherit" problem-solving mechanisms from those who've suffered from depression in the past, most of which only increase the risks of developing depression. For example, a young person whose parent had developed depression but opted to keep silent about it could also walk down that path, thus increasing the risk.

7. Depression confines you to a lifetime of drugs

The truth: - You may never need to take depression medications to deal with this condition. Additionally, people with depression do not have to depend on antidepressants for the rest of their life in order to overcome the problem. In fact, drugs could only be necessary for a few days or weeks, based on the assessment of your medical practitioner.

There are other myths that have been advanced in the past, most of which can be scary and effective in increasing the stigma associated with depression. Always seek to learn the truth as a way of demystifying these myths.

Chapter 7: Ways to Avoid Depression Relapse

Once you've gone through a period of depression and have received treatment, the last thing you want to see is a relapse. Depression is ugly and unpleasant something you wouldn't wish on your worst enemy. Unfortunately, many sufferers of depression do experience relapses during recovery, especially when proper measures are not taken to avoid this problem. Below are some steps to take in order to live a healthy life and to avoid a relapse.

Avoid overloading your mind

The world has become a busy place, and many people consider that they will fail if they do not engage in a lot of activities. While it is important to be busy, filling your hands with too much could soon become a trigger for depression relapse. A sense of devastation can create stress and this can increase the risk of depression relapse. It is good to know your limits and create a balance when dealing with life issues. Doing so will help to keep you safe. Think about the simplicity of the daily lives of your ancestors or grandparents – and how they did just fine and how their lives were just as valuable and worthwhile. Try to be more like that.

Exercise regularly

Exercise is part of the natural remedy for depression. They can also be very helpful in preventing cases of depression relapse. Regular exercising can work as a remedy for stress and helps lighten depression and related symptoms. Studies have suggested that exercises that have or are coupled with meditative focus could also help to prevent cases of depression and relapse.

Develop healthy thinking skills and a positive attitude

Looking at life positively and developing a positive attitude can help overcome some depression triggers. Therapies such as Cognitive Behavioral Therapy are geared to help a depression patient develop a more positive outlook towards him or herself, and life in general. Although these therapies do not work on their own, people can use the lessons learnt to develop a positive outlook on issues, thus overcoming real and imaginary factors that are likely to cause depression. No matter what may have stirred or triggered depression, developing a positive mentality could work as a shield against a relapse. Don't read too much from nothing and, again, avoid judging yourself or a situation harshly simply because you have noted a negative aspect in it.

Eat proper diet

What you eat will help you to maintain your physical and mental well-being. For example, foods rich in omega-3, low in fat and rich in folic acid, can help in the development of a positive mood. Other things that could help relieve stress include green, black and herbal teas, vegetables and fruits. Additionally, avoid alcohol and lower the amount of caffeine-containing foods as part of your healthy eating program.

Work on your social life

Many people who slip into depression normally lead a lonely or isolated life prior to and during the time of their sickness. However, building healthy and trusted relationships can work not only to help recovery but also in preventing cases of depression relapse. Do not be an island in yourself, instead, connect with others and enjoy their love and help.

Stop self-blaming

Self pity and other cases of being too conscious about small issues in your life could trigger depression symptoms. Whether you are going through a low season or have much on your plate, it is prudent to avoid blaming yourself for everything in your life.

Rest and sleep properly

Sufficient rest and sleep are necessary for recovery and prevention of depression relapse. Sleep will help regulate your moods, while also rejuvenating you both mentally and physically. People with insomnia are more likely to relapse into depression than those who sleep well at night. Sleep is essential for your health and you must never consider it a waste of time. Many people think that sleeping through the night is a sign of laziness. This is incorrect and one of the great lies of our present, busy world. Sleeping and resting properly will help your mind and body to function effectively.

It is also important to take some time to do the things that make you happy. In most cases, people with depression cut back on such activities. This can work against your recovery process. To live a healthy life and avoid a relapse, you should come up with a list of activities that makes you feel happy about life, and engage in them whenever you notice some warning signs or feel overwhelmed. Whether it is swimming or talking to a friend, travelling or engaging in a certain hobby, try to give yourself time and make the most out of such moments. Remember, healing from depression is a process. You would not want to get back to the dungeon again, so keep yourself healthy and be happy.

Conclusion

Depression can leave you drained of all hope, energy and drive. It can push you deeper into places which you would never want to imagine. If you are already suffering from this problem, the best thing will be to get up and seek help. You must never sit down to pity yourself, or live in denial. You are not in depression because you are weak and useless, no! You are going through an unfortunate period in your life and this is not the end. The best thing is to seek professional help and to talk to your spiritual leaders and those who care and love you deeply.

In addition, you can prevent depression by watching for any warning signs, especially those that are likely to leave you deeply stressed. Stress can lead to depression, and dealing with or managing stress will go a long way towards keeping you safe. Depression can be chronic in some people, and if you are suffering from this disorder the best thing you can do is to work towards recovery. If you are recuperating, the best thing is to ensure that you have completed your treatment and that you work towards preventing a recurrence or a relapse. Relapse is normally defined as suffering a new episode of the mental disorder less than 6 months after a treatment for acute depression, while recurrence is any new episode that occurs 6 months or more after the initial treatment. No matter where you are, your well-being is very important and you must not give up the will to live.

In case you are facing a depression relapse or recurrence, make a point of talking to a therapist, psychiatrist or a doctor as soon as possible. If you feel at all emotionally overwhelmed, or are tackling episodes of stress, the same steps will be necessary. Don't wait for the problem to worsen, take a step early and get the help you need. In many cases depression can be prevented and, in all cases, it can be treated successfully, helping you live a normal, healthy life.

Remember, treating depression takes time, but nothing is impossible if you put the effort in and make the right decisions for yourself every day. I hope you found this book helpful! If you did, I would be grateful if you would take a moment to leave a review on Amazon.

Made in the USA
Columbia, SC
02 January 2022

53144043R00030